Table of Contents

CHAPTER 1: THE BASICS OF TRAVELING TO MEXICO

Visas, Flights, and First Impressions

Introduction

The allure of Mexico is undeniable. With its rich culture, diverse landscapes, and warm hospitality, it's a destination that beckons travelers from around the globe. But before you can sip margaritas on a sun-soaked beach or explore ancient Mayan ruins, there are some logistical hurdles to clear. This chapter serves as your comprehensive guide to the basics of traveling to Mexico, covering everything from visa requirements to flight bookings and what to expect upon arrival.

Types of Tourist Visas

Visa-Exempt Countries

If you're fortunate enough to hail from a visa-exempt country, your entry into Mexico is relatively straightforward. You can enter the country and stay for up to 180 days without needing a pre-approved visa. However, this doesn't mean you can board a flight and land in Mexico without any documentation. You'll still need to fill out a Forma Migratoria Múltiple (FMM), commonly known as the Mexican Tourist Card, either during your flight or upon arrival. As of the publishing date of this book you no longer required to fill this out. This is subject to change at any time.

Action Steps:

1. **Check Visa-Exempt Status**: Before you even book your flight, check if your country is on the visa-exempt list. This information is available on the Mexican Consulate's website. Knowing your visa status will help you plan your trip more effectively.

2. **Passport Validity**: Ensure that your passport is valid for at least six months from your planned date of return. Immigration authorities may deny entry if your passport is nearing its expiration date.

3. **Filling Out the FMM**: During your flight, airline staff will distribute FMM forms. Fill this out carefully, as errors can cause delays at immigration. Keep this form safe throughout your trip, as you'll need to present it when you leave Mexico.

Case Study: John, a U.S. citizen, planned a three-month backpacking trip across Mexico. He assumed that being from a visa-exempt country meant he didn't need to worry about any paperwork. However, upon landing, he realized he had misplaced his FMM form. The immigration process was delayed, and he had to pay a fine to get a new form.

Pre-Approved Visas

If you're not from a visa-exempt country, you'll need to apply for a visa before traveling to Mexico. While this process requires more preparation, it's generally straightforward if you know what to expect.

Action Steps:

1. **Schedule an Appointment**: The first step is to schedule an appointment at the nearest Mexican consulate. Appointments can fill up quickly, especially during peak

travel seasons, so it's advisable to do this well in advance.

2. **Gather Required Documents**: Each consulate may have slightly different requirements, but generally, you'll need the following:
   - A valid passport
   - Proof of accommodation (hotel bookings or a letter from a host)
   - Financial statements or proof of funds
   - Travel itinerary
   - Passport-sized photos
   - Visa application form

3. **Attend the Appointment**: On the day of your appointment, arrive early and bring all the required documents. You'll submit these and may have a brief interview where you'll be asked about your travel plans, financial stability, and other relevant details.

4. **Pay the Fee and Wait**: After submitting your application, you'll need to pay a non-refundable visa application fee. The time it takes to process your visa can vary, so it's best to apply well in advance of your planned departure date.

Case Study: Maria, a citizen of the Philippines, decided to visit Mexico for a cultural exchange program. She scheduled her consulate appointment two months in advance and diligently gathered all her documents. However, she overlooked the financial statements requirement, assuming her scholarship would cover it. At the consulate, she was informed that without proof of funds, her application couldn't proceed. Maria had to reschedule her appointment, delaying her visa and subsequently her travel plans.

Recommended Website: Mexican Consulate

Booking Your Flight: Best Practices

Budget and Timing

The cost of flights to Mexico can vary significantly based on several factors, including the time of year, the airline, and how far in advance you book. Generally speaking, flights are cheaper during the off-peak season, which for Mexico is from May to mid-December.

Action Steps:

1. **Set a Budget**: Before you even start looking for flights, it's crucial to set a budget. Knowing how much you're willing to spend will help you narrow down your options and make the search more manageable.

2. **Use Comparison Websites**: Utilize flight comparison websites like Skyscanner, Kayak, or Google Flights to get an overview of the price ranges for your desired travel dates. These platforms aggregate prices from various airlines and booking websites, giving you a comprehensive view of your options.

3. **Be Flexible with Dates**: If your travel dates are flexible, you can compare prices on different days to find the most cost-effective options. Generally, flying mid-week is cheaper than flying on weekends.

Case Study: Emily, a budget traveler, wanted to spend her summer vacation in Mexico. She started looking for flights three months in advance and used Skyscanner to compare prices. By choosing to fly on a Wednesday instead of a Friday, she saved over $100 on her round-trip ticket.

Layovers

Direct flights are undoubtedly the most convenient, but they're also generally the most expensive option. If you're traveling on a budget, flights with layovers can be a cost-effective alternative, although they come with their own set of challenges.

Action Steps:

1. **Check Layover Duration and Location**: When considering flights with layovers, always check the duration and location of the layover. A layover that's too short may not give you enough time to clear customs and catch your connecting flight, while a layover that's too long can make your journey unnecessarily tedious.

2. **Transit Visas**: Some countries require a transit visa for layovers, even if you don't plan to leave the airport. Always check the visa requirements for the country where you'll be laying over to avoid any unpleasant surprises.

Case Study: Ahmed, traveling from India to Mexico, opted for a cheaper flight with a layover in the United States. He assumed that since he wouldn't be leaving the airport, he wouldn't need a visa. However, upon checking, he realized that the U.S. requires a transit visa for all layovers. Ahmed had to scramble to get a transit visa, adding stress and additional cost to his travel plans.

Next, we'll discuss what to expect upon your arrival in Mexico, covering topics like immigration and customs procedures.

First Impressions: Airports and Customs

Arrival and Immigration

The moment your plane touches down in Mexico, the next phase of your journey begins. You'll disembark and follow the signs to the immigration area, where you'll present your travel documents and go through a few formalities before you're officially allowed to enter the country.

Action Steps:

1. **Have Documents Ready**: Before you get off the plane, make sure you have all your necessary documents in an easily accessible place. This includes your passport, visa (if applicable), and the FMM form you filled out earlier. Fumbling for documents can delay the process and create unnecessary stress.

2. **Follow Signs to Immigration**: Airports in Mexico are generally well-signposted in both Spanish and English. Follow the signs to the immigration area and join the queue that applies to you—either Residents or Visitors.

3. **Answer Immigration Questions**: Once it's your turn, you'll present your documents to the immigration officer. They may ask you questions about the purpose of your visit, where you'll be staying, and how long you plan to be in Mexico. Answer honestly and clearly.

Case Study: Sarah, a solo traveler from Australia, landed in Cancun for a two-week vacation. She had all her documents ready and answered the immigration officer's questions confidently. The process was smooth, and she was through immigration in less than 20 minutes.

Customs

After clearing immigration, you'll proceed to the baggage claim area to collect any checked luggage. From there, you'll move on to customs, where you'll need to declare any items that are subject to duty or restrictions.

Action Steps:

1. **Collect Your Luggage**: Follow the signs to the baggage claim area and collect your luggage. Make sure to check that you've picked up the correct bags to avoid any mix-ups.

2. **Declare or Not to Declare**: Before exiting, you'll pass through customs. If you have items to declare, you'll need to fill out a customs declaration form and may be subject to further inspection. If you have nothing to declare, you can pass through the "Nothing to Declare" lane.

3. **Exit the Airport**: Once you've cleared customs, you're officially in Mexico! Follow the signs to the exit, where you can catch a taxi, shuttle, or other forms of

transportation to your accommodation.

Tip: Always keep a digital copy of your important documents, such as your passport, visa, and any other permits, stored securely in the cloud or on a USB drive. This can be a lifesaver if you lose your physical copies.

Case Study: Carlos, traveling from Brazil, had a bottle of premium cachaca that he wanted to gift to a friend in Mexico. Unsure if he needed to declare it, he decided to take the "Nothing to Declare" lane. Customs officers selected him for a random check and found the bottle. Carlos had to pay a fine for not declaring the item.

CHAPTER 2: WHERE TO STAY AND HOW TO GET AROUND

Accommodations, Public Transport, and Car Rentals

Introduction

Once you've navigated the initial hurdles of visas and flights, the next big questions are where you'll stay and how you'll get around. Mexico offers a wide range of accommodation options, from luxury resorts to budget hostels, and an equally diverse array of transportation choices. This chapter aims to guide you through these options, helping you make informed decisions that align with your travel style and budget.

Accommodations

Hotels and Resorts

Mexico is home to some of the world's most luxurious hotels and resorts, particularly in tourist hotspots like Cancun, Playa del Carmen, and Los Cabos. These establishments offer top-notch amenities, including private beaches, gourmet dining, and spa services.

Action Steps:

1. **Set a Budget**: Determine how much you're willing to spend per night on accommodations. This will help narrow down your options.

2. **Use Booking Platforms**: Utilize hotel booking platforms like Booking.com, Expedia, or Airbnb to compare prices and amenities.

3. **Read Reviews**: Always read reviews from other travelers to get a sense of the quality of the hotel or resort.

Case Study: Lisa and Mark, a couple from the UK, decided to splurge on a five-star resort in Cancun for their honeymoon. They used Booking.com to compare options and read reviews to ensure they were getting the best value for their money. Their research paid off, and they had an unforgettable experience.

Hostels and Budget Accommodations

For travelers on a budget, Mexico offers a plethora of hostels and budget hotels. These are particularly common in backpacker-friendly destinations like Tulum, Oaxaca, and Mexico City.

Action Steps:

1. **Research Locations**: Look for hostels or budget hotels in safe neighborhoods that are close to the attractions you want to visit.

2. **Check Amenities**: Even budget accommodations can offer valuable amenities like free Wi-Fi, breakfast, or lockers. Check what's included in the price before you book.

3. **Read Reviews**: As with hotels, always read reviews to gauge the quality of the hostel or budget hotel.

Case Study: Emily, a solo backpacker, was traveling through Mexico on a shoestring budget. She used Hostelworld to find hostels and always read reviews to ensure she was staying in safe and clean places. Her research allowed her to travel affordably without sacrificing her comfort or safety.

Local Transportation

Public Transport

Mexico's public transportation system is generally reliable and affordable, especially in larger cities like Mexico City, Guadalajara, and Monterrey. Buses and metro systems are the most common forms of public transport.

Action Steps:

1. **Get a Transport Card**: In cities with a metro system, consider getting a prepaid transport card to make commuting easier.

2. **Use Apps**: Utilize apps like Google Maps or Waze to plan your route and get real-time updates on public transport.

3. **Be Cautious**: Always keep an eye on your belongings, as pickpocketing can be an issue, especially during rush hours.

Case Study: Alex, a digital nomad, spent a month in Mexico City. He bought a prepaid Metro card and used Google Maps to navigate the city's extensive public transport system. By doing so, he was able to explore the city efficiently and affordably.

Taxis and Rideshares

Taxis are widely available in Mexico, but it's essential to ensure you're using a registered taxi service to avoid scams. Rideshare apps like Uber and Didi are also available in many cities and are generally considered safe and reliable.

Action Steps:

1. **Use Reputable Services**: Always use registered taxis or trusted rideshare apps.

2. **Confirm the Price**: Before starting the ride, confirm the price or make sure the meter is running to avoid being overcharged.

3. **Share Your Ride**: If using a rideshare app, consider sharing your ride details with a trusted contact for added safety.

Case Study: Sophia, traveling in Cancun, needed to get from her hotel to the airport. She used Uber and shared her ride details with a friend. The experience was seamless, and she felt secure knowing someone knew her whereabouts.

Car Rentals

Renting a car offers the most flexibility but comes with its own set of challenges, such as navigating unfamiliar roads and dealing with local traffic laws.

Action Steps:

1. **Check Requirements**: Make sure you meet the age and documentation requirements for renting a car in Mexico.

2. **Get Insurance**: Always opt for comprehensive insurance coverage when renting a car.

3. **Familiarize Yourself with Local Laws**: Before hitting the road, familiarize yourself with local traffic laws to avoid fines or other issues.

Case Study: John and his family rented a car to explore the Yucatan Peninsula. They made sure to get comprehensive insurance and spent some time studying local traffic laws, which made their road trip enjoyable and stress-free.

CHAPTER 3: EXPLORING MEXICO'S DIVERSE REGIONS

From Beaches to Mountains, Cities to Jungles

Introduction

Mexico is a country of incredible diversity, both in its landscapes and its cultural offerings. Whether you're drawn to the sun-soaked beaches of the Yucatán Peninsula, the bustling energy of Mexico City, or the serene beauty of the Sierra Madre mountains, there's something here for every type of traveler. This chapter aims to guide you through some of Mexico's most iconic regions, helping you decide where to go based on your interests and what you hope to get out of your trip.

The Yucatán Peninsula

Beaches and Resorts

The Yucatán Peninsula is home to some of Mexico's most famous beaches, including Cancun, Playa del Carmen, and Tulum. These destinations are perfect for travelers looking for a classic beach vacation complete with luxury resorts, water sports, and vibrant nightlife.

Action Steps:

1. **Choose Your Beach**: Each beach has its own unique vibe. Cancun is known for its party atmosphere, Playa del

Carmen offers a mix of relaxation and entertainment, and Tulum is famous for its bohemian, laid-back feel.

2. **Book Activities**: From snorkeling in cenotes to jet-skiing on the ocean, the Yucatán Peninsula offers a wide range of water activities. Book in advance during peak seasons.

3. **Explore Nearby Islands**: Consider taking a day trip to nearby islands like Isla Mujeres or Cozumel for a different beach experience.

Case Study: Laura and her friends were looking for a beach destination that offered both relaxation and adventure. They chose Playa del Carmen, where they enjoyed the beach during the day and explored the bustling Fifth Avenue at night. They also took a day trip to Cozumel to go snorkeling.

Mayan Ruins

The Yucatán Peninsula is also rich in history, home to some of the most well-preserved Mayan ruins, including Chichen Itza, Coba, and Tulum.

Action Steps:

1. **Plan Your Visit**: Decide which ruins you want to visit and whether you'll go independently or as part of a tour.

2. **Get There Early**: These sites can get crowded, especially Chichen Itza. Arrive early to beat the crowds and the heat.

3. **Hire a Guide**: Consider hiring a local guide to gain deeper insights into the history and significance of these ancient sites.

Case Study: Mike, a history enthusiast, visited Chichen Itza as part of a guided tour. He arrived early and was able to explore the site before it got too crowded. The guide provided valuable historical context that enriched his experience.

Mexico City: The Heart of the Nation

Culture and History

Mexico City, the country's capital, is a bustling metropolis that offers a unique blend of modernity and history. From the ancient ruins of Teotihuacan to the contemporary art scene, the city is a cultural powerhouse.

Action Steps:

1. **Visit Museums**: Don't miss the National Museum of Anthropology, Frida Kahlo Museum, and the Palace of Fine Arts for a deep dive into Mexican culture and history.

2. **Explore Historic Sites**: Visit the Zócalo, the city's main square, and the nearby Templo Mayor, an ancient Aztec temple.

3. **Take a Day Trip**: Consider a day trip to Teotihuacan to explore the ancient pyramids.

Case Study: Rachel, an art lover, spent a week in Mexico City and dedicated each day to exploring different aspects of the city's culture. She visited several museums and took a day trip to Teotihuacan, making her trip both enriching and diverse.

Food and Nightlife

Mexico City is also famous for its culinary scene, offering everything from street food to gourmet dining experiences.

Action Steps:

1. **Try Street Food**: Don't miss out on trying tacos, tamales, and churros from street vendors.

2. **Dine in Style**: For a more upscale dining experience, consider restaurants like Pujol or Quintonil, which offer modern takes on traditional Mexican cuisine.

3. **Experience Nightlife**: From trendy bars in Polanco, Condesa and Roma to traditional mariachi music in Plaza Garibaldi, the city offers a vibrant nightlife.

Case Study: Carlos, a foodie, made it his mission to explore Mexico City's culinary scene. He balanced his meals between street food and high-end restaurants, giving him a well-rounded culinary experience.

The Pacific Coast: Surf, Sand, and Seafood

Beach Towns

The Pacific Coast is known for its laid-back beach towns like Puerto Vallarta, Sayulita, and Zihuatanejo. These destinations offer excellent surfing, fishing, and a more relaxed atmosphere compared to the Yucatán Peninsula.

Action Steps:

1. **Choose Your Destination**: Each town has its own unique charm. Puerto Vallarta is known for its vibrant arts scene, Sayulita for its surfing, and Zihuatanejo for its fishing.

2. **Try Water Activities**: Besides surfing, you can also go whale watching, fishing, or snorkeling.

3. **Enjoy Seafood**: The Pacific Coast is famous for its seafood. Don't miss out on trying dishes like ceviche and grilled fish.

Case Study: Emma and Tom, an adventurous couple, chose Sayulita for its surfing opportunities. They took surfing lessons and enjoyed the town's relaxed vibe.

CHAPTER 4:
PRACTICAL MATTERS

Safety, Healthcare, and Staying Connected

Introduction

While Mexico offers a wealth of experiences and attractions, it's essential to address some practical matters to ensure a smooth and enjoyable trip. This chapter will guide you through important topics like safety, healthcare, and how to stay connected during your travels.

Safety in Mexico

General Precautions

While Mexico is generally a safe country for tourists, it's always wise to take certain precautions to ensure your safety.

Action Steps:

1. **Research Your Destination**: Before you go, research the safety situation in your chosen destination. Some areas may have higher crime rates than others.

2. **Keep Valuables Secure**: Use a money belt or a secure backpack to keep your valuables safe, especially in crowded areas or public transport.

3. **Stay Alert**: Always be aware of your surroundings, particularly in unfamiliar areas or during nighttime.

Case Study: Sarah, a solo female traveler, made sure to research the safety situation in each city she planned to visit. She used a money belt to keep her valuables secure and always stayed alert, ensuring a safe and enjoyable trip.

Emergency Contacts

Knowing whom to contact in case of an emergency can be crucial.

Action Steps:

1. **Save Local Emergency Numbers**: Save the local emergency numbers, including police, medical services, and your country's embassy, on your phone.

2. **Know the Location of the Nearest Embassy**: In case of serious issues, it's good to know the location of your country's embassy or consulate.

3. **Have a Backup**: Always have a backup plan and share your itinerary with a trusted contact back home.

Case Study: Mike, while traveling in Mexico, lost his passport. Because he had saved the contact information for his country's embassy, he was able to quickly get assistance and resolve the issue.

Healthcare in Mexico

Medical Precautions

Mexico has a good standard of healthcare, especially in larger cities, but it's always better to be prepared.

Action Steps:

1. **Get Travel Insurance**: Always travel with comprehensive travel insurance that includes medical coverage.

2. **Pack a First Aid Kit**: Carry a basic first aid kit with essentials like band-aids, antiseptics, and any prescription medications you may need.

3. **Know Where to Go**: Familiarize yourself with the

location of the nearest hospital or clinic in your chosen destination.

Case Study: Emily, who has a chronic medical condition, made sure to carry all her prescription medications and also knew the location of the nearest hospital. This preparation gave her peace of mind during her travels.

Staying Connected

Internet and Communication

Staying connected while traveling in Mexico is generally easy, thanks to widespread internet access and good mobile coverage.

Action Steps:

1. **Get a Local SIM Card if needed**: For affordable data and local calls, consider getting a local SIM card upon arrival. A lot of companies such as AT&T include Mexico in most phone plans. Please check with your provider if you will have service in Mexico.

2. **Use Wi-Fi**: Most hotels, restaurants, and public spaces offer free Wi-Fi, but always make sure the network is secure before connecting. We do suggest using a VPN to protect your data.

3. **Stay in Touch**: Use apps like WhatsApp or Skype to stay in touch with friends and family back home without incurring high international calling fees.

Case Study: Carlos, a digital nomad, got a local SIM card for data and local calls and used secure Wi-Fi networks for work. He also used WhatsApp to keep in touch with his family, making staying connected easy and affordable.

CHAPTER 5: WRAPPING IT UP

Your Ultimate Guide to a Memorable Mexican Adventure

Introduction

You've navigated through the complexities of visas and flights, explored accommodation and transportation options, delved into the diverse regions of Mexico, and equipped yourself with practical knowledge on safety, healthcare, and staying connected. Now, as we wrap up this comprehensive guide, let's revisit some key takeaways and offer some final tips for your journey.

Key Takeaways

1. **Planning is Crucial**: Whether it's visas, flights, or accommodations, planning in advance can save you time, money, and stress.

2. **Mexico is Diverse**: From the beaches of the Yucatán Peninsula to the cultural richness of Mexico City, the country offers a wide range of experiences to suit every traveler's interests.

3. **Safety First**: Always prioritize your safety by staying alert, keeping valuables secure, and knowing whom to contact in case of emergencies.

4. **Healthcare Matters**: Travel with comprehensive insurance and a basic first aid kit to ensure you're prepared for any medical situations.

5. **Stay Connected**: A local SIM card and secure Wi-Fi networks will keep you connected during your travels.

Final Tips

1. **Be Open to New Experiences**: While planning is essential, be open to spontaneity. Sometimes the best experiences are the ones you didn't plan for.

2. **Respect Local Customs**: Always be respectful of local customs and traditions. This not only enriches your travel experience but also fosters positive interactions with locals.

3. **Savor the Moment**: Whether you're watching the sunset over the Pacific Ocean or exploring ancient ruins, take the time to savor the moment. These are the experiences that will make your trip truly unforgettable.

4. **Keep a Travel Journal**: Documenting your experiences can be a wonderful way to reflect on your journey and share it with others.

5. **Have Fun**: Ultimately, the goal is to enjoy yourself. With the right preparation and mindset, your trip to Mexico can be a memorable adventure filled with incredible experiences.

CHAPTER 6:
OBTAINING
RESIDENCY IN MEXICO

Navigating the Path to Becoming a Mexican Resident

Introduction

Whether you're drawn to Mexico's warm climate, rich culture, or affordable cost of living, the idea of making this vibrant country your permanent or semi-permanent home can be appealing. However, the process of obtaining residency can be complex and requires careful planning and understanding of the legal requirements. This chapter aims to guide you through the different types of residency options, the application process, and other key considerations to help you make an informed decision.

Types of Residency

Temporary Resident Visa

A Temporary Resident Visa is suitable for those who wish to stay in Mexico for more than 180 days but less than four years. This visa can be renewed annually.

Action Steps:

1. **Check Eligibility**: Ensure you meet the financial requirements, which usually involve proving a stable income or significant savings.

2. **Gather Documents**: Collect all required documents, such as bank statements, proof of employment, and any other supporting materials.

3. **Apply at Consulate**: The application for a Temporary Resident Visa must be submitted at a Mexican consulate in your home country.

Case Study: Jane, a retired American, applied for a Temporary Resident Visa to spend her winters in Mexico. She gathered all her financial documents and successfully applied at the Mexican consulate in the United States.

Permanent Resident Visa

A Permanent Resident Visa is for those who wish to live indefinitely in Mexico. You can apply for this after four years of holding a Temporary Resident Visa or two years if you are married to a Mexican citizen.

Action Steps:

1. **Check Eligibility**: Similar to the Temporary Resident Visa, financial stability is crucial. Additional requirements may apply.

2. **Gather Documents**: Assemble all necessary documents, including proof of your time spent on a Temporary Resident Visa if applicable.

3. **Apply in Mexico**: Unlike the Temporary Resident Visa, the application for Permanent Residency is usually submitted within Mexico.

Case Study: Carlos, originally from Spain, spent four years in Mexico on a Temporary Resident Visa. He then successfully transitioned to a Permanent Resident Visa by meeting all financial and documentation requirements.

The Application Process

1. **Preparation**: Research and gather all required

documents. Some documents may need to be apostilled or notarized.

2. **Submission**: Submit your application and documents to the appropriate Mexican consulate or immigration office.

3. **Interview**: An interview may be required to assess your application.

4. **Approval and Card Issuance**: Once approved, you'll receive your resident card, which must be renewed based on the type of visa you have.

Key Considerations

1. **Legal Assistance**: The process can be complex; consider hiring a legal advisor familiar with Mexican immigration laws.

2. **Financial Planning**: Ensure you meet the financial requirements not just for the application but for your long-term stay in Mexico.

3. **Integration**: Think about your long-term plans for integrating into Mexican society, including learning the language and understanding the culture.

CHAPTER 7: EMBRACING THE MEXICAN LIFESTYLE

Language, Customs, Food, and Festivals

Introduction

Once you've navigated the legalities of obtaining residency, the next exciting phase is immersing yourself in the rich and diverse culture of Mexico. This chapter aims to provide you with insights into the language, customs, food, and festivals that make Mexico a unique and vibrant place to live.

Language: The Heart of Communication

Spanish Basics

While many people in tourist areas speak English, learning Spanish is invaluable for deeper integration into Mexican society.

Action Steps:

1. **Take a Course**: Consider enrolling in a Spanish language course either online or in-person.

2. **Practice Daily**: Use language exchange apps or converse with locals to practice your Spanish.

3. **Immerse Yourself**: Watch Spanish movies, read Spanish books, and listen to Spanish music to improve your language skills.

Case Study: Maria, who moved to Mexico from the United States, took a three-month intensive Spanish course and practiced speaking with her neighbors. This helped her feel more at home and facilitated her daily interactions.

Customs and Etiquette

Social Norms

Understanding the social norms and etiquette can go a long way in making your transition smoother.

Action Steps:

1. **Greetings**: Learn the common forms of greetings, which often involve a handshake, hug, or kiss on the cheek.

2. **Punctuality**: While social events may have a more relaxed approach to time, it's essential to be punctual for formal occasions and appointments.

3. **Respect for Elders**: Older individuals are highly respected in Mexican culture, and it's customary to offer them your seat in public transport or let them go ahead in lines.

Case Study: John, a retiree from Canada, quickly learned the importance of punctuality when he missed his first appointment with a local doctor. He made sure to arrive early for all subsequent appointments.

Mexican Cuisine: A Culinary Journey

Must-Try Dishes

Mexican cuisine is a rich tapestry of flavors, textures, and aromas. From tacos and enchiladas to mole and chiles en nogada, the food is as diverse as the country itself.

Action Steps:

1. **Explore Local Markets**: Visit local markets to try fresh

produce and traditional dishes.

2. **Learn to Cook**: Consider taking a cooking class to learn how to prepare Mexican dishes at home.

3. **Dine Out**: Explore a variety of restaurants to experience the full range of Mexican cuisine.

Case Study: Emily, a food blogger, took a cooking class in Oaxaca to learn how to make mole. She documented her experience on her blog, sharing the rich history and complexity of this iconic dish.

Festivals: Celebrating Mexican Culture

Popular Festivals

Mexico is known for its colorful and lively festivals, such as Day of the Dead, Cinco de Mayo, and the Guelaguetza.

Action Steps:

1. **Plan Ahead**: Some festivals attract large crowds, so it's advisable to book accommodations and transportation in advance.

2. **Participate**: Don't just be a spectator; immerse yourself in the festivities by participating in dances, parades, or other activities.

3. **Learn the Significance**: Understanding the cultural or historical significance of a festival will enrich your experience.

Case Study: Alex and Lisa, a couple from Germany, visited Mexico during the Day of the Dead. They took the time to learn about the festival's significance and even participated in a local parade, making their experience truly memorable.

CHAPTER 8: FINANCIAL PLANNING FOR LIFE IN MEXICO

Banking, Taxes, Cost of Living, and Investments

Introduction

Moving to a new country involves not just cultural adjustments but also financial planning. Understanding the banking system, being aware of tax obligations, and having a grasp on the cost of living are crucial for a smooth transition. This chapter aims to provide you with a comprehensive guide to managing your finances while living in Mexico.

Banking in Mexico

Opening a Bank Account

Having a local bank account can make your financial life much easier, from receiving payments to handling day-to-day expenses.

Action Steps:

1. **Choose a Bank**: Research and select a bank that offers services tailored to your needs.

2. **Gather Required Documents**: Typically, you'll need identification, proof of address, and possibly a financial reference to open an account.

3. **Visit the Bank**: Most banks require you to open an

account in person. Make an appointment and bring all necessary documents.

Case Study: Robert, a freelance writer, opened a bank account with a Mexican bank that offered online services, making it easier for him to manage his finances from anywhere.

Taxes in Mexico

Understanding Your Obligations

If you're residing in Mexico for more than 183 days a year, you're considered a tax resident and are subject to Mexican taxation on your worldwide income.

Action Steps:

1. **Consult a Tax Advisor**: Speak with a tax advisor familiar with both your home country's and Mexico's tax laws.

2. **Register with Tax Authorities**: You'll need to register with the Mexican tax authorities and obtain a tax identification number.

3. **File Taxes**: Understand the deadlines and requirements for filing your tax returns in Mexico.

Case Study: Sarah, who runs an online business, consulted a tax advisor to understand her tax obligations in both the United States and Mexico. She registered with the Mexican tax authorities and files her taxes annually.

Cost of Living

Budgeting for Everyday Life

The cost of living can vary significantly depending on your location and lifestyle.

Action Steps:

1. **Research Costs**: Look into the cost of housing, utilities, groceries, and other essentials in your chosen location.

2. **Create a Budget**: Based on your research, create a monthly budget to manage your expenses effectively.

3. **Adjust as Needed**: Your first few months will be a learning experience. Be prepared to adjust your budget as you get a better understanding of your actual expenses.

Case Study: Emily and Tom moved from New York to Playa del Carmen and found that their monthly expenses were about 30% lower, allowing them to enjoy a higher quality of life.

Investments

Opportunities and Risks

Mexico offers various investment opportunities, from real estate to the stock market.

Action Steps:

1. **Consult Financial Advisors**: Before making any investments, consult with financial advisors familiar with the Mexican market.

2. **Understand Regulations**: Be aware of any legal restrictions or requirements for foreign investors.

3. **Diversify**: Consider diversifying your investment

CHAPTER 8: FINANCIAL PLANNING FOR LIFE IN MEXICO

Banking, Taxes, Cost of Living, and Investments

Introduction

Managing your finances in a new country can be a complex task. This chapter aims to simplify that process, covering everything from banking and taxes to the cost of living and investment opportunities in Mexico.

Banking in Mexico

Opening a Bank Account

Having a local bank account can facilitate your financial transactions in Mexico.

Action Steps:

1. **Choose a Bank**: Research and select a bank that meets your needs.

2. **Gather Required Documents**: Usually, you'll need identification and proof of address.

3. **Visit the Bank**: Most banks require you to open an account in person.

Case Study: Robert, a freelance writer, chose a bank with robust online services, making it easier for him to manage his finances.

Taxes in Mexico

Understanding Your Tax Obligations

Your tax obligations in Mexico depend on your residency status. Mexican residents are taxed on worldwide income, while non-residents are taxed only on income sourced in Mexico.

Action Steps:

1. **Consult a Tax Advisor**: Speak with a tax advisor familiar with Mexican tax laws.

2. **Determine Your Residency**: Understand whether you qualify as a resident or non-resident for tax purposes in Mexico.

3. **File Taxes Accordingly**: If you're a resident, you'll be taxed on worldwide income. If you're a non-resident, you'll be taxed only on Mexican-sourced income. (This is highly debated)

Case Study: Sarah, an online business owner, consulted a tax advisor to understand her tax obligations in Mexico and the United States. She determined that she was a non-resident for tax purposes in Mexico and filed her taxes accordingly.

Cost of Living

Budgeting for Everyday Life

The cost of living varies depending on your location and lifestyle in Mexico.

Action Steps:

1. **Research Costs**: Investigate the cost of housing, utilities, groceries, and other essentials.

2. **Create a Budget**: Formulate a monthly budget based on your research.

3. **Adjust as Needed**: Be prepared to modify your budget as you become more familiar with your expenses.

Case Study: Emily and Tom found that their monthly expenses were about 30% lower in Playa del Carmen compared to New York, allowing them to enjoy a better quality of life.

Investments

Opportunities and Risks

Mexico offers various investment opportunities, from real estate to the stock market.

Action Steps:

1. **Consult Financial Advisors**: Speak with financial advisors familiar with the Mexican market.

2. **Understand Regulations**: Be aware of any legal restrictions or requirements for foreign investors.

3. **Diversify**: Consider diversifying your investment portfolio to mitigate risks.

Case Study: David, a real estate investor, consulted with financial advisors and legal experts before purchasing property in Mexico. His diversified investment strategy included both real estate and local stocks, providing him with multiple income streams.

CHAPTER 9: NAVIGATING HEALTHCARE IN MEXICO

Understanding the System, Insurance, and Finding Providers

Introduction

Healthcare is a critical aspect to consider when planning to live in a new country. Mexico offers various healthcare options, ranging from public to private services. This chapter aims to guide you through the healthcare landscape in Mexico, helping you make informed decisions for your well-being.

The Healthcare System

Public vs. Private

Mexico has both public and private healthcare systems. The public system is affordable but may have longer wait times, while the private system offers quicker service but at a higher cost.

Action Steps:

1. **Research**: Understand the pros and cons of both systems to determine which suits your needs.

2. **Registration**: If opting for public healthcare, you'll need to register with the Mexican Social Security Institute

(IMSS).

3. **Facility Tour**: Visit a few healthcare facilities to get a feel for the services offered and the general environment.

Case Study: Linda, a retiree, chose to use both public and private healthcare. She registered with IMSS for routine check-ups and opted for private healthcare for specialized treatments.

Health Insurance

Options and Coverage

Health insurance is highly recommended, especially if you plan to use private healthcare services.

Action Steps:

1. **Compare Plans**: Research and compare different health insurance plans to find one that meets your needs.

2. **Understand Coverage**: Make sure you understand what is and isn't covered by your chosen plan.

3. **Purchase**: Once you've made your choice, go through the purchasing process, which may include a medical examination.

Case Study: Mark, a digital nomad, chose an international health insurance plan that provided comprehensive coverage, including emergency evacuation, as he often travels for work.

Finding Healthcare Providers

Doctors, Specialists, and Hospitals

Finding a healthcare provider that you're comfortable with is crucial.

Action Steps:

1. **Ask for Recommendations**: Consult friends, family, or online expat communities for recommendations.

2. **Check Qualifications**: Ensure that the healthcare provider has the necessary qualifications and experience.

3. **Initial Consultation**: Schedule an initial consultation to assess whether you're comfortable with the provider.

Case Study: Emily, who has a chronic condition, asked for recommendations and did thorough research before choosing a specialist. She scheduled an initial consultation and was satisfied with the level of care provided.

CHAPTER 10: LONG-TERM PLANNING FOR LIFE IN MEXICO

Setting Goals, Building Community, and Enjoying Life

Introduction

Once you've navigated the initial hurdles of moving to Mexico—like obtaining residency, understanding the financial landscape, and securing healthcare—the next step is to focus on long-term planning. This chapter aims to guide you through setting goals, building a community, and ultimately, creating a fulfilling life in Mexico.

Setting Goals

Personal and Professional

Whether it's learning the language, starting a business, or buying a home, setting clear goals will give your life direction.

Action Steps:

1. **Identify Goals**: Make a list of both short-term and long-term goals.

2. **Prioritize**: Rank your goals in order of importance and feasibility.

3. **Create a Plan**: Develop a step-by-step plan to achieve each goal.

Case Study: John, an entrepreneur, set a goal to start a local business within two years. He prioritized this goal and created a detailed business plan.

Building Community

Social Circles and Networking

Building a strong social circle and professional network can greatly enhance your life in Mexico.

Action Steps:

1. **Join Groups**: Participate in social or professional groups related to your interests.

2. **Attend Events**: Go to community events, workshops, or seminars to meet new people.

3. **Be Open**: Be open to forming relationships with people from different backgrounds.

Case Study: Lisa, a graphic designer, joined a local art community and attended various workshops. This not only enriched her social life but also expanded her professional network.

Enjoying Life

Leisure and Well-being

Living in Mexico offers a plethora of opportunities to enjoy life, from beautiful beaches to rich cultural experiences.

Action Steps:

1. **Explore**: Take time to explore different regions of Mexico.

2. **Engage in Activities**: Whether it's surfing, hiking, or attending a local festival, engage in activities that bring you joy.

3. **Maintain Balance**: While it's essential to work and

achieve goals, don't forget to take time for yourself.

Case Study: Emily and Tom, who moved from New York, make it a point to explore a new region of Mexico every three months. This has not only enriched their lives but also given them a deeper appreciation for the country.

EPILOGUE

The Journey Ahead

As we come to the end of this comprehensive guide, it's important to remember that the journey to living your dream life in Mexico is just beginning. You've equipped yourself with the knowledge and tools needed to navigate the complexities of travel, residency, financial planning, and healthcare in this beautiful country. But the real adventure starts now, as you apply what you've learned to your own unique circumstances.

The Power of Preparedness

Being prepared is more than just a motto; it's a lifestyle choice. The information in this book aims to prepare you for various scenarios you might encounter in Mexico. Whether it's choosing the right visa, understanding the tax implications, or selecting a healthcare provider, being prepared will make your transition smoother and more enjoyable.

Building Your Community

Remember, you're not alone on this journey. There are countless others who have walked this path before you and many who will follow. Take advantage of this collective wisdom. Engage with the community, both online and offline, to enrich your experience and to offer your own insights to those who come after you.

Your Personal Roadmap

This book serves as a roadmap, but it's up to you to drive the journey. Set your goals, both short-term and long-term, and revisit them regularly. Life is dynamic, especially in a new country, and your plans will need to be equally adaptable.

Final Thoughts

Mexico is a land of incredible diversity, rich culture, and endless opportunities. It offers a quality of life that many expats find fulfilling and enriching. As you embark on this exciting new chapter, keep an open mind and a willing spirit. The challenges will be part of the adventure, and the rewards will be well worth the effort.

Thank you for allowing this book to be a part of your journey to living the Mexican dream. Here's to new beginnings, exciting adventures, and a life well-lived in Mexico.

ARE YOU READY TO LIVE THE MEXICAN DREAM?

Mexico—a land of vibrant culture, stunning landscapes, and endless opportunities. Whether you're planning a short trip or considering long-term residency, this comprehensive guide is your ultimate roadmap to a life well-lived in one of the world's most captivating countries.

Inside This Book, You'll Discover:
Essential Travel Tips: From visas to accommodations, get all the information you need for a successful trip.

Safety Guidelines: Equip yourself with the knowledge to stay safe and secure in various regions of Mexico.

Financial Planning: Navigate the complexities of banking, taxes, and investments like a pro.

Healthcare Insights: Understand your healthcare options and how to choose the best for you.

Long-Term Planning: Learn how to set personal and professional goals, build a community, and enjoy a fulfilling life in Mexico.

Why Choose This Book?
Actionable Steps: Each chapter ends with practical action steps and case studies to help you apply what you've learned.

Expert Advice: Benefit from expert insights and tips that will save you time, money, and unnecessary stress.

Comprehensive Coverage: This all-in-one guide addresses every aspect of traveling and living in Mexico, making it the only resource you'll need.

Embark on an exciting new chapter of your life with "Living the Mexican Dream: A Complete Guide to Travel and Residency." Whether you're a seasoned traveler or a first-timer, this book is your passport to a successful and enriching experience in Mexico.

27308495R00027